My *Life* in *Poetry* and *Love*

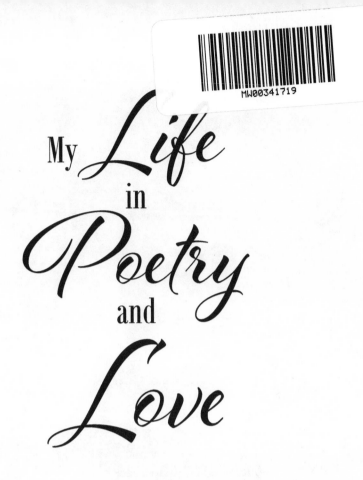

Volume 1

Gail Bard Coussoule

ISBN 978-1-0980-7831-7 (paperback)
ISBN 978-1-0980-7832-4 (digital)

Christian Faith Publishing, Inc.
832 Park Avenue
Meadville, PA 16335
www.christianfaithpublishing.com

Printed in the United States of America

My life ebbs and flows like the tides of the sea as
new generations come, replacing the old.

Contents

Preface

I, Gail Bard Coussoule, am an authoress of prayers and poetry based on a lifetime of giving love to many who need the Lord's help, inspiration to aspire to be the best one can be in time of need, to be well when there seems no hope, and to treasure life where one began as an infant and where one ends after a lifetime of learning that where the Lord places us is where He intended us to be.

I grew up in the Berkshire Hills of Adams, Massachusetts, the hometown of Susan B. Anthony. I knew her descendants and I loved every moment of my life there.

One day in 1964, words came to me very suddenly. I dropped my apron and ran to my desk to respond to my heart, which was dictating words about my beautiful baby girl. No matter where my life led me, the inspiration to write never stopped for those needing my love.

Enjoy my life, my love of the Lord, my dedication to family, friends, and those who serve the Lord in any capacity.

> I am dedicated to those who read
> and love the great gifts that God gives
> us at birth to those who share the
> sorrows, struggles, and successes of others.

May God bless you and may you enjoy the many blessings described in this book.

Country

A Poetic Photo of the Berkshires

The stars shine brightly overhead
on this Berkshire summer night.
Fireflies invade the distance
the air has lost that bite.
I think of days, so long ago,
when I, a child, ran free
Through fields of daisies, and tall grass
just the family dog and me.
Summertime was special, then—
It meant that we could play
Out of doors and into dark
there was no school next day.
The swimming hole was not too far
the woods were very near
We could think of things to do
we ventured without fear.
How very fast the summers went
this time of so much pleasure
Family picnics, so much love
A memory to treasure.

The days are growing shorter
Fall is in the air
Leaves are turning color
Time for the County Fair.
Now the leaves begin to fall
to rake and pile high—

then jump right in and cover up,
Lay still and face the sky.
While lying there in leaves so brown
we'd watch the clouds float by
Imagining that they were sheep—
We were children, you and I.
The air has now grown crisply cold
Autumn now has flown
Another season is upon us
the nights have longer grown.
Winter starts, the ground is white—
It's like a fairy tale
Christmas will soon be upon us
Holiday thoughts prevail.
Days are now so short
and North winds blow so strong
sleds and shovels are in sight
Berkshire winters were so long.
The coming days are longer
temperatures now are easing
Sights and sounds around us now
are beginning to be more pleasing.
I felt the earth becoming soft
It had begun to thaw
The bite of winter is gone once more
It is no longer raw!
The sun is higher in the sky
the ice and snow are gone
I cannot wait to shed my coat
Oh, Spring, it's you I long!
As I step out of <u>my</u> front door
the birds warble their tune.
It beckons me to run and play
Spring arrives very soon!
Feelings uplift to happy ones
there is no trace of gloom

Neighbors emerge once more to chatter
erasing thoughts of doom.
Look about and up above
the trees have reached full bloom
The fragrance I inhale
Are the blossoms' own perfume.
Oh, God, I thank thee many times
over these many years
To have grown up in the Berkshire Hills
to have abandoned my childhood fears.

Yes, Cousin Gen, we are aware
awaiting each special season
To feel the lonely winter nights
to cry without a reason.
We knew the joy that was to come
as winter season gave birth
To greet the new born infant, Spring
welcoming Mother earth—
Yes, welcoming her with arms outstretched
so invigorated were we
To start our chores, <u>so</u> refreshed
with <u>new</u> vitality.
And Special Cousin, very soon,
your doors will open wide
To beckon all the fragrant air,
to welcome it inside.
And, too, you'll find your feelings,
alive and all aglow
Reviving all our childhood dreams
we dreamed <u>so</u> long ago.
Perhaps our special visit
through God's heavenly grace
Will <u>one</u> <u>day</u> see us reunited
embracing face to face.
And though my Daddy cannot be

<u>with</u> <u>us</u> for that day—
He's watching all our letters cross;
if he were here, he'd say—
"Gen and Gail, your family bond,
those who're left are few
I am watching day and night
and I am proud of you!
So Gen and Gail, keep the love
the Bards have left to all
Our Berkshire family memories
are the fondest to recall!"

Card by Bard
3/23/95

America—The Right to Vote

I voted today and I pray God heard,
what is in my heart, His Holy Word.
Protect our country, your greatest gift.
Restore the wrongs; may our spirits lift.

The future looks cloudy for those who rule—
Let not our young be easy to fool!
They know not our documents, nor do they care—
could it send the country to complete despair?

Will your miracles, my Lord, soon arrive
to save your people that we may survive?
I pray for this land, the land of my birth—
for ALL that behold its golden worth.

Take it back, dear Jesus, it's not theirs to spoil—
Bless all in our land who labor and toil.
America's riches are many, indeed—
We have your blessings to fulfill each need.

Our talents have made us all that we are.
America's heart reaches near and afar.
I will end my poem on this final note—
NEVER take for granted the "Right to Vote!"

Card by Bard
11/2/10

His Mystery

God works in <u>mysterious</u> ways
Consulting no one, He plans our days.
He sends us forth from break of dawn,
As we arise with our first yawn—
We rise, it seems, with clouded heads—
Pull up the spread and make our beds.
Into the kitchen for our morning blessing,
We say our prayers, get on with dressing.
We're ready, Lord, this day to face,
Prepared to set our daily pace.
Whatever career He's planned for me,
I'll be the best I can possibly be.
No matter what you've chosen, Lord,
I'll do it well; I'll <u>not</u> be bored.
A doctor's pledge is made to heal;
A priest and nun are vowed to kneel.
A father's pride is in his work—
Whether lawyer, farmer, dean, or clerk.
A mother holds a sick child's hand,
Then glances at her wedding band.
Her lifelong work is giving love,
With patience sent from God above.
God's <u>mystery</u> message becomes so clear;
He calls His flock from far and near—
To share the talents spread over all—
To do His work, to heed His call.
"Share what I gave to each of you—

Have love and pride in all you do.
For when I call you home to rest
and you have passed your earthly test;
No more, dear child, will you despair
or wonder if <u>someone</u> will care."
God keeps His promise of dreams untold,
Bringing us to His heavenly fold.
But <u>only</u> if we do each deed
Serving those who are in need—
Spreading His word in <u>mysterious</u> ways,
through His love, for <u>ALL</u> <u>our</u> <u>days</u>.

Card by Bard
7/19/90

Kindness

Kindness is showing a lovely thought
It's doing helpful things.
Deeds are never done for naught
When to a face a smile it brings.
Extend your hand to those in need
It is a privilege and a must
Doing for others, taking the lead—
helping the poor gain trust.
We have not forgotten those,
who suffer day and night;
for if we have the door will close
locking them in plight.
Put yourself right in their place,
I'm speaking of someone in trouble.
Would their problem be hard to face?
Would it seem to grow and double?
Surely you would look around
for someone's hand to hold.
You'd look for a kind face and a sound,
be he young or be he old.
Yes, kindness takes on many forms
It's caring for our brothers—
We can face a life of storms
if we live and work with others.

Card by Bard
9/2/70

Our Prayer for Peace, Humanity, and Love

Prayers in number now increase
by folks who yearn and pray for peace.

"Please put the world in capable hands
Leaders of strength who can meet all demands."

Place your faith in God, without Him, we're through;
America needs Him, indeed we do.

The world heard a warning in Garabandal;
Mother Mary appeared to <u>warn</u> of our fall.

Will we listen to Her and start changing our ways;
or will we <u>do</u> <u>as</u> <u>we</u> <u>please</u> for the rest of our days?

God is not happy but one chance remains
to cling to Him just as Mary explains.

Bringing peace and love to this world in turmoil;
the snake of Satan is beginning to coil.

Once He springs it's too late to look back with regret
and the fate that WE'VE chosen will surely be met!

Card by Bard
7/2/70

Family

A Father's Day Greeting

As Dad snuggles back in his easy chair
We can tell he relaxes there.
He's worked so hard his whole life long
He forgets the world and all that's wrong.
More deserving a Dad, there never could be
He's done so much for his family—
This day set aside to honor him now
Is but little to do to show him how—

1. All he has done we can never forget
2. All his advice has been our best bet
3. All that we do is what he has taught
4. Most of our tools are the tools he has bought
5. All of the standards we use are high
6. And they've all been set by this very great guy

Happy Day to Dad, from all of us, too,
Just keep right on being that wonderful you!

Card by Bard
6/16/70

A Father's Day Prayer

A father to our children
No one could take his place.
During their years of growing
they shared his fond embrace—
For projects well completed
for good deeds so well done—
Very often he would say
"I'm proud my daughter and my son!"
Today his children stand alone
though they need not Dad's advice—
For every single move they make
nor do they need his wife.
But in their hearts they know their Dad
is never far away.
They only need to phone him
to know what he would say—
"Son, please stay the course
as your grandpa told to me;
Daughter, lend a helping hand,
for success, it holds the key!"
"Love the world around you
be positive and pray—
Give your hearts to one and all
Keep going come what may."

Dad, you are the best there is
You raised your children fine.
And from your wife and lover
I'm thankful you are mine.

My love this Father's Day,

Your loving wife

Card by Bard
6/14/96

A Message to All Mothers

Be patient my friend, for this is your life—
to be a mother and kind, loving wife.
We have <u>chosen</u> a life full of grief and despair,
It can make a woman want to tear out her hair!
But my friend take advice that so long you have heard
I would not lie, take heed of my word.

There's a challenge to meet; you may not see it yet.
But it slowly appears, the older they get.
You can pass to your children much of what <u>you</u> have learned
Keep your poise while you teach, their respect you'll
have earned.
For they sense, <u>even</u> <u>now</u>, just how much parents care—
by our touch, by our smile, by our eyes; it's <u>all</u> there.

The emotions we're "<u>hiding</u>" are there on <u>display</u>—
just as big as the signs that light up Broadway.
When times get you down and you feel you will "bust"—
And you must talk to someone, a friend you can trust—
Just remember these words, they are all very true
They are made for <u>ALL</u> mothers, and that includes you!

"We are <u>HUMAN</u>, <u>INTELLIGENT</u>,
and need <u>UNDERSTANDING</u>
For the chores in our day are far more demanding—
We are "raising" the future scientists and teachers
Ranchers, doctors, engineers, and preachers.

If we fail in our work, a generation will fall,
So you see, we have the toughest job of them all.
So we, too, are entitled to some time of our own
to think, or paint, or just be alone.
We, too, want to cry or smile or scream—
We, too, have the right to fulfill each dream.
So part of our job is to teach those we love—
In voices as soft as the peace of a dove.
They must learn they must give as well as receive.
It's a rule to accept as well as believe.
They will grow up knowing the rule of "share"—
They will try in their play to always be fair.
They will know and expect that this mother so true
Is entitled to privacy and dignity, too.
We don't ask for much in this work of "giving;"
Just a space so tiny to do some living.
You cannot feel guilty at one time or another—
It's essential to the work of a well-rounded mother."

Card by Bard
12/17/71

Apart

There's no sadder time than a family apart,
the lull in life simply tugs at the heart.
For years they were home, keeping Mom and Dad busy;
they were in they were out, Lord, what a tizzy!
Mark grew from a boy to a handsome young man.
Lisa followed him daily completing his plan.
To school they traveled to learn what they could;
the reason for this, "they knew that they should."
They did not delight in their time of learning.
they longed for advancement, achievement, and earning.
To do this they knew they must follow through;
they proceeded to college and started anew.
With the world in their hands, they set in motion
tasks and chores that would flood an ocean.
Years have gone by, they labored hard
their new assistant was Grandmother Bard.
They told themselves they could not miss
with people who cared like Grandmother Cis.
Mom and Dad ache, though they do what they can
for this magnificent lady and ambitious man.
With pride do they speak of their daughter and son
admiration and tributes they truly have won.
Does success and hardship go hand-in-hand?
Do they determine what life will demand?
Must the mountain they climb be so steep
obstructing the vision of dreams they reap?
Must the sweat and blood that have turned their wounds red

equal the tears we know they have shed?
Is time the answer to a dream come true
when there's no consolation for feeling blue?
Does thinking the positive, failure dispel,
forsaking mistakes on which one must not dwell?
Should focus on future, on plans, and on dreams
be added to daily new plans and schemes?
Must brave little souls so determined to learn
have to be subjected to people who spurn?
Spurn their efforts, their heartfelt work each day;
is that what it takes, leading one to dismay?
Resolved once again, must a challenge we meet;
we will not bow to succumb to defeat!
The final blow will we strike to stay.
We will ask for help as we kneel to pray.
God grant this family so far apart
that they be sustained within the heart.
Sustained by the love and the bonds so real
they could not be broken if struck by steel.
God watch over Mark, our valiant son.
Bless Lisa, our daughter who is second to none.
Let faith, hope, and love be the answer to all
as they start once again to answer this call.
Let the smiles of success to a happy face bring;
Let it rise, dear Lord, like the flowers of Spring.
And if this plan was meant to be——
this family apart will unite happily.

To my family
Love, Mom

Card by Bard
02/06/86

Dedicated to Our Fathers

Fathers come in all shapes and sizes,
Some are full of delightful surprises.
Some are young, some are old—
Some are shy and some are bold.

The man we honor today is he
that devoted life to you and me.
He gave us shelter from the storm—
kept us feeling safe and warm.

Dad would place his family first,
Their successes made him burst—-
With pride and love for every member
All the year right through December.

Can you remember your first bike,
Vacations, mountains, or a hike?
Can you remember long ago
you hurt your knee or stubbed your toe?

You had a toy that he must fix
That's when you were barely <u>SIX</u>!
Dad was always there to aid,
These memories will <u>never</u> fade.

When it hurt, he wiped our tears;
He soothed away our many fears.
A bad report, remember when—
The teacher scolded—you were TEN!

Do you remember your first date?
Dad had warned, "Now don't be late!"
He wasn't trying to be mean,
You were "pushing" SWEET SIXTEEN!

College days are on the way
Dad's the one who had to pay.
He wants his kids to be secure,
Free from problems to endure.

Graduation, Dad was there,
Smiling face, emotions bare—-
Tears ran down his face this day—
"You made it child, I'm proud to say!"

"Find a job, do not delay."
Dad's advice would surely pay.
"Find a mate, don't be alone."
We can tell just by his tone—-

Dad's life with Mom is so complete,
It's time to find someone to meet.
Wedding day due to arrive
Now you are—TWENTY-FIVE!

A baby due, sent from heaven,
You are now—TWENTY-SEVEN!
The years go by, it is our turn
To father, guide, teach, and learn.

Somehow no one can take <u>his</u> place
<u>Our</u> <u>father</u> <u>with</u> the gentle face.
The man we love and so adore,
No one could ever ask for more.

Happy Father's Day, my love.
May God send blessings from above.
Affection, love from your wife,
<u>You</u> <u>are</u> <u>the</u> <u>one</u> who changed <u>my</u> life.

Card by Bard
06/13/86

To Fifi's Loving Parents

On her way to wherever it is that good doggies go when
their time has come to depart, Miss FiFi stopped by to see her
Auntie Gail. She had something on her mind. She wanted me
to tell you in my own way just how special her folks were. You
see, she knew how you felt about her, but she wanted you to
know how she felt about you.
And we want you to know we share your sorrow in her passing.

Fifi

Dear family,
If I could talk, you'd hear me say
"It is my time, I cannot stay."
I'll miss your warm and tender touch
I loved you both <u>so</u> <u>very</u> <u>much</u>.

You shared your warm and loving home
You never set me free to roam.
You groomed me at the "House of Charm"—
<u>Protected</u> <u>me</u> from hurt and harm.

My favorite hour was "four" to eat
followed by my favorite "treat."
I knew that you would never fail
but I could only wag my tail.

For I wanted you to know
How <u>good</u> you were to make it so!
I <u>will</u> not tell you not to mourn
I know you both feel sad and torn.

<u>Please</u> remember <u>what</u> we've shared
A pet who loved two who cared.
<u>Think</u> of me with my red bow—
<u>my</u> black coat with that <u>special</u> glow.

<u>Think</u> of my eyes so faithful and true

as they'd understand each deed you'd do.
We <u>shared</u> a mutual bond of love
as warm as the summer sun above.

<u>Dear</u> <u>family</u>, we're <u>only</u> as far apart
As the constant beat of a loving heart.

Affectionately,
Fifi

Card by Bard
4/1/86

Godmother

On Baptism Day, in her arms she takes
her sister's child so dear
And now before God this vow she makes
To love her and remain ever near.

As the child now looks back to those days gone by,
her memory recalls many things—
the affection bestowed when at times she would cry
and tears to my eyes it <u>still</u> brings.

How I wonder with amazement the <u>patience</u> that she had
with each glass of milk I would spill
How I wonder <u>why</u> she <u>never</u> got mad
as she <u>patiently</u> would just refill.

She consented to sit while Mother and Dad
were going through much of their strife;
A normal childhood she saw that I had,
to <u>her</u> I owe <u>much</u> of my life.

Her help and goodness fulfilled that vow
<u>many</u> times more than her share
and the warmth of her love I feel even now
of <u>this</u> I <u>hope</u> she's aware.

Can <u>she</u> remember the trips that we took
every Sunday in the hills?

As Uncle Ed would bait his hook,
what <u>wonderful</u> childhood thrills!
I want her to know that I'll <u>never</u> forget
and <u>thank</u> <u>her</u> from <u>deep</u> in my heart
There's not a moment I'll <u>ever</u> regret
even now that we're miles apart.

A godmother true she always has been,
a pillar of strength was a must—
She gave of herself again and again
and, of course, she obtained all my trust.

As you know by now, I've been speaking of <u>you</u>—
and <u>I</u> <u>must</u> have been first in line
when God gave out godmothers, He <u>surely</u> knew
that there <u>was</u> <u>none</u> <u>finer</u> than mine!

Card by Bard
01/21/70

Happy Anniversary to Two Special People

Your <u>special</u> day is once more here,
the memories shared by <u>two</u> are clear.

For years have a way of slipping by
when the <u>two</u> in love see eye to eye.

And when <u>two</u> in love share every day
the marriage thrives in a <u>special</u> way.

You are this couple of whom I write—
<u>Always</u> hold this love in a <u>special</u> light.

Card by Bard
09/18/72

Happy Birthday, Mother

Happy Birthday wishes, Mother
Across the miles with love for you—
There has never been another
Who can do the things you do.

You have earned the name of mother
through your love and tender care.
Each deed you do exceeds the other
making you beyond compare.

Bless the hands that worked so hard
bless the face sincere and sweet
Bless the words within this card
bless your heart with every beat.

God grant you health to do each thing
you've longed so much to do
and may the joys that follow bring
the best in life to you.

Card by Bard
07/06/70

Heart of Gold

To Lisa Marie from Mom

Have you ever heard of a "Heart of Gold?"
Is it real, can you touch it, a sight to behold?
Can a human fulfill what seems like a dream;
a person or image with energy extreme?
Each day that I face, the larger the task;
there are at times, it's too much to ask!
Suddenly, the image appears from nowhere—
a smile on her face, crowned with beautiful hair.
"I'm here to help you, not too much to do;
my heart wants to help because I love you!"
That's the angel I speak of, the "Heart of Gold;"
I yearned many years for this daughter foretold—
by God, my Savior, who willed her to me—
He said, "For a lifetime, I'll share her with thee."
"She's our daughter to share, then heaven will call;
my gift to your family because I love you all!"

Blessings,
Your Savior

Card by Bard
07/31/18

Mom and Me

Dedicated to the lady I love and adore, my mom

If that lady could live forever,
Or just as long as me—
If I could see or hear her
Just think how life would be.
The comfort she would offer me
whenever I feel stress—
How many times she needed me,
Only God could guess!
The years are swiftly flying by
Two lonely hearts are blue
Mother, dear, you'll <u>never</u> know
How <u>much</u> I've needed you.
Keep strong between each visit
for I live to see your smile
And though it isn't often—
and it's only for a while—
We stop to steal a weekend
or maybe just a day,
It's like picking up some sunshine
to take upon our way.
That smile and love you give us

Warms our hearts and home
And stays within our being
wherever we shall roam.

My love, your daughter

Card by Bard
10/27/77

Son

It isn't every day
that someone comes along
who's tall and handsome, muscular,
with character that's strong.

It isn't every day
that God from heaven sends
a human that can do it all—
on no one else depends.

It isn't every day
a man completes each task
with a plethora of knowledge;
one only has to ask.

The man that we are speaking of
that God has sent our way
is <u>our</u> <u>son</u> that we so love,
<u>and</u>, it <u>isn't</u> every day!

Card by Bard
2/14/96

The Secret Message of Mothers

Mother's Day—May 10, 1970

The life of a mother is devotion and care
for the children she bore that they reach their goals fair.
For their sakes she would say, "No"
though it hurt deep inside—
Can you guess all the times
that she turned and cried?
Mother's decision seemed strange at the time
"Why did she say, 'no' when it was 'only a dime'?"
"That isn't too much to ask for, not now,"
"I'll ask for more later, if she will allow!"
But Mother was firm and we're glad that she was—
there is a good reason for all that she does.
Her love is unending as childhood we leave
Her message remains: TO GIVE MORE THAN RECEIVE.
The wisdom in her words we're just finding out
She left nothing unsaid that would cast any doubt.
It takes many years to penetrate clear
All the messages Mother gave year after year.
We can say many words about Mother, it's sure—
She is charming, and wise, delightful and pure—
She's our counselor, nurse, teacher, and cook
Mother's complexity would fill a complete book.
She asks for nothing in return for all this

except, "Do not go through life being remiss."
And so it is fitting that there is Mother's Day
To say "thanks" to these ladies on this tenth day of May.

Card by Bard
04/29/70

To My Husband, Jack

The man that I love could only be you,
with a heart that is big and one that is true.

Soft eyes, bright smile, on a kind loving face,
bring memories to mind that are hard to erase.

Only you have the hands that I love to hold;
Only you can bring joys as the years will unfold.

And last, but not least, your embrace and your kiss,
make our marriage complete, wedded joy and bliss.

With all my love,

Card by Bard
11/2/67

God's Healing Grace

A Prayer for Healing

A prayer for you is said this day
to speed your progress on its way.

May God's light shine, may His love be
All it takes to strengthen thee.

Do what the doctors say you must;
above all, keep God in your trust.

Faith and trust will guide you through;
our prayers will always be with you.

Card by Bard
11/15/70

Blessings

In spring, we see the flowers grow
In winter, we see the blowy snow
In summer, we see the lake so blue
In fall, we see the shades of hue.

God gave us <u>all</u> these wonderful things
the thrill the change of season brings.
He gave us the animals, birds and bees,
the sky so blue and the seven seas.

What precious gifts are these from Him
Who made the mountains, rock, and limb.
<u>How</u> <u>rich</u> are we in many ways
<u>How</u> <u>blessed</u> we are through all our days!

Card by Bard
12/8/69

Humbled

God, I'm sorry that I've hurt you
I suffer deep inside
For all the things I say and do
This grief I cannot hide.

Please accept my sorrow now
I need to kneel each day
To beg forgiveness as I bow
My heart and head to pray.

I need your strength to guide me
as I walk this road in life,
Your kingdom has a golden key
Attained through daily strife.

Things don't always go my way
I sometimes fail the test
I shout my anger during the day
Though I've tried to do my best.

It seems to spoil the good I've done
I wonder how I've slipped
How weak I was, where should I run
I've fallen again and tripped.

Help me pick up the pieces, Lord
Don't let me linger in sin
Keep me from always being bored
Your love, I'll surely win.
I'm sorry, for I love you so
Forgive my thoughtless deed
I want my soul with love to grow
Jesus, Lord, it's You I need.

Card by Bard
8/29/80

My Healing

Take me into your gentle arms;
Press me to your breast
Until you do, my dear Lord,
I cannot feel my best.
Your Sacred Heart is beating;
I hear its beckon call
telling me, "You can't give up;"
such pain I can't recall!
The need arises each new day;
I find I'm feeling blue.
I'm digging deep within myself;
I feel my faith renew!
It's very strong, I'm holding tight,
I draw my strength from prayer.
Please, dear Savior, save me soon;
don't let this be despair!
I can't give up; I must go on—
Jesus showed us how
To bear our hurts, to heal our pain;
I'll make this vow <u>right now</u>—
Please, Savior, never leave me
for I need your guiding light—
To lead me forth to better days
to fight this awesome fight!

And when I find this battle won
and I'm the victor blessed—
Remember the night you held me tight
near to your heart and breast.

Card by Bard
08/06/18

Heaven

A Little Peek at Heaven!

Find me a rainbow, find me a dream,
find me a forest with a beautiful stream.
Show me a lark, show me a dove
show me the creatures God made with His love.

Neither fortune nor fame can interest me here—
I am going away to a land without fear.
A land far away, yet totally near
where man will <u>never</u>, <u>again</u>, shed a tear.

It's reserved for the blessed who carry His will
from the day they were born 'til they cross "o'er the hill."
At the end of this life is a rest so supreme—
a reward for our efforts fulfilling this dream.

Card by Bard
07/28/71

Happiness Is...

Happiness is all too short
It passes you quickly by;
Learn to enjoy it; <u>never</u> resort
to gloom, despair, and die.

If it were not for all the heartaches—
and God gave us both, you see,
to appreciate what it takes
to bring happiness to you and me.

He gave us work, then gave us play
He gave us dark, then gave us light
He made some cry, and some so gay
He made some blind and some with sight.

He knew that we must have both extremes
to make perfect happiness
to help us fulfill our finest dreams
through bitterness and success.

Happiness is all of these things
wrapped into our daily lives;
Replacing the hate with love it brings
the pleasures that one derives.

Card by Bard
01/27/70

Mary, Our Queen

I'm closest to heaven when I visit our shrine—
speaking with Mary and her Son, so divine.
Miracles abound when to Mary we pray—
Her answers are **never** too far away.
For her Son denies **NOT** what His Mother will ask;
intercession by Mary will accomplish the task.
There "**is**" no favor too great or too small—
They <u>hear</u> our prayers; they answer our call.
Mary Queen of the Universe, now our national shrine,
sent by the Lord as a heavenly sign—
Placed in the heart where Walt Disney World towers
as a home for tourists amidst beauty and flowers.
<u>Jesus</u> **chose** this land that would be the best—
He appointed His Mother to take care of the rest.
"**F. Joseph Harte, your mission's begun!**"
"**Yes**," was his answer—"**Thy will be done.**"
Priest, Director, and then to be—
"Monsignor;" our hearts are grateful to thee.
Years of labor and years of toil
'til they finally turned the earthen soil—
Out of the ground Mary's dream rose
where millions now gather, <u>and</u> <u>where</u> <u>prayer</u> <u>flows</u>.
It **is** **sacred**; **it** **is** **hallowed**; built in her name—
Mary, our Queen, whom we love and acclaim.

Card by Bard
06/01/07

The Silence of the Lord

How does our invisible LORD
remain hidden from our eyes?
How <u>does</u> He perform His miracles—
one only can surmise.

He goes about His work each day
<u>not</u> <u>ever</u> to be seen—
We, the benefactors of His will,
some way, His truths do glean.

His presence is all around us—
He makes <u>not</u> a sound—
He walks and speaks so "<u>silently</u>"—
<u>YET</u>, His miracles abound.

Do you recognize His footsteps,
Though He leaves <u>not</u> <u>one</u> footprint?
Do you listen to His voice each day
as He leaves a tiny hint?

He gives you inspiration
then, pollenates His love—
He goes about His work
with the "<u>silence</u>" of a dove.

Our hearts and minds are focused—
our eyes miss not a clue—
He tells us in so many ways
"My children, I love you!"

"Go about your tasks, dear ones;
complete each special plan—
Always say these special words—
Dear LORD, I know I can!"

The life you lead will be fulfilled—
the peace of mind well earned—
The gifts and lessons from our God
will now have been well learned!

Love, from your Savior

Card by Bard
04/05/15

Holiday

A Deeper Meaning

Holly, wreaths, and mistletoe
symbols of Christmas cheer
Gladness, Yule time spirits ring
the mood is crystal clear.

Snow is falling, bells are ringing
they toll from steeples high.
Carolers sing the songs we love
Christmas Eve and morn are nigh.

The feeling in our hearts is big;
we strive to help each other
We all must do our parts to help,
Sister, Dad, Mom, and Brother.

Then finally on Christmas morning
when the awaited day arrives,
it is not the gifts that we have received
that will bring joy to our lives.

We are celebrating the birthday
of our Savior Jesus Christ
He was born on earth to make us free
His life He sacrificed.

So on Christmas Day we all must try
to have God in our hearts—
And, let us work for peace on earth
before the New Year starts.

Card by Bard
11/19/68

Christmas is Giving

It's such a cold and lonely night
The people come to see the sight—
A King is born a humble birth
His destiny: to rule the Earth.
From that night forth until this day
We honor Him a special way—
By giving, by sharing, by loving each friend
By caring for those who long hours do spend.
The sick and the poor, the needy and such
For they have so little, and we have <u>so</u> much.
Our Christmas is finer for deeds we have done
The love of the Lord we surely have won.
Our hearts become bigger as Christmas arrives
And the pleasures one <u>gives</u> are the ones he derives!

Card by Bard
12/01/72

Our Christmas Day Prayer

Happy Birthday, Little Jesus
We celebrate your birth
Redeemer, baby, brought to us
In Bethlehem on earth.

How humble your beginning
How mankind saw you fall
But God had served His purpose
For you to save us all.

As we wish a Merry Christmas
To our loved ones and each friend,
Why can't we bring our thoughtfulness
All year, from start to end?

Please, dear Lord, hear our prayers
We offer, so sincere
For peace on Earth, good will toward men
And God's blessings this New Year.

Card by Bard
12/25/78

Thanksgiving Day Prayer
(1971)

We thank thee with a humble heart
for blessings bestowed this year.

We thank thee, God, for food and health
for courage to proceed without fear.

This bread now placed before us
reminds us there might not be—

A chance to express our love and thanks,
Father, were it not for thee.

Card by Bard
11/16/71

The Crucifixion and Resurrection of Our Lord, Jesus Christ

Jesus dies to free all mean
And sorrow fills our hearts—
but we look ahead to Easter, when
the time for rejoicing starts.

How this scourging must have hurt each limb—
Can you feel His Mother's loss?
Do you want to share His pain with Him
As they nail Him to the cross?

His eyes toward heaven try to see
Blood trickles as He pleads—
"Father, hast thou forsaken me,
I have completed all your deeds."

As He dies the sky becomes all black
And suddenly He is to know,
As thunder loud begins to crack
That His Father's wrath will show.

The time has come to take Him down
And place Him in the tomb
And remove the thorns that formed His crown,
this man from Mary's womb.

Christ rises bright on Easter morn
His followers' hearts are gay.
As blessed an event as the day He was born
Never more in this tomb shall He lay.

His death has shown what it means to <u>give</u>
The pattern is <u>so</u> very clear
His rising teaches us <u>how</u> to live
With the thought that heaven is near.

Blessed are they whose faith is unshaken
who stand firm in times of strife
For it is they who shall be taken
Into the kingdom of eternal life.

Card by Bard
3/5/70

The True Meaning of Christmas

It's time again to share our glee
as this holy time draws near,
With those who trim our Christmas tree
and those who are so dear.

The holly and the mistletoe
may make our season bright,
But the meaning, as we truly know,
is of a baby born this night.

He came to us from God above,
so He could show the way
To express the meaning of true love,
as we live and work each day.

A Merry Christmas to everyone,
May you be blessed in every way,
A New Year filled with joy and fun,
A very happy holiday.

Card by Bard
12/2/66

About the Author

Gail's early years include a love of English and business courses that culminated in her graduation as a Pro Merito student. She moved onto working as a stenographer-typist for the engineers in the Ordnance Division of the General Electric Company who developed the guidance system for the Polaris Missile. She went on to marry her husband, John, of sixty-one years, before moving to Connecticut, where they raised their two children. Gail now resides in Florida with her husband and daughter.